Elijah Helps the Widow

The Story of Elijah and the Drought
1 Kings 17:1–16 for children

Written by Nanette Thorsen-Snipes
Illustrated by Susan Morris

CONCORDIA PUBLISHING HOUSE · SAINT LOUIS

Elijah came from Gilead—
A prophet righteous and bold.
He bravely spoke about a drought
That God above foretold.

"No rain will fall upon the land,"
Elijah told the king.
The prophet then went on ahead
And found a place for hiding.

"Hide in Kerith Ravine," God said.
"The ravens will feed you there."
Elijah did what God had said.
And had food and water to spare.

But one day Elijah's brook dried up;
The water was gone, gone, gone!
So God sent him to a widow
Who lived in a faraway town.

Elijah watched as she gathered sticks
And said, "Please, do you mind,
Bringing me something cold to drink;
A cake of bread would be kind."

She turned to go, to grant his wish,
Then said in apology,
"I have no bread, only some flour
And oil for my son and me."

With sorrow then, she hung her head,
With tears, began to cry.
"I fear this is our very last meal.
We'll eat and then we'll die."

"Don't be afraid," Elijah said.
"Go with your son and abide.
But first make one small cake for me—
The Lord, our God, will provide.

"Your jar of flour will not be gone;
The jug of oil will remain.
Neither one will ever run out
Until God above sends rain."

The widow then went on her way
And did as Elijah said.
With the pan, she heated the oil
And cooked a piece of bread.

The widow woman came to give
Elijah his cake of bread.
And when he finished the last of it,
"Is there some for us?" she said.

In faith, she'd used all that she had
To give to the man that day.
And as she turned to go back home,
She heard the prophet say:

"Just as the Lord sent the ravens
To feed me night and day,
The Lord will send you oil and flour,
So cast your worries away."

In fact, God said there would be food
Each day for mother and boy.
And for Elijah the prophet—
God's word was a thing of joy.

And the flour was not used up;
The oil did not go dry.
Elijah had spoken God's word in faith—
"The Lord for you will provide!"

This message is for all believers—
Made clear to each of us.
God will provide for all our needs.
In Him we can always trust.

Dear Parents,

In a drought-stricken land, God responded to Elijah's need. Elijah encouraged the widow to believe as he did—that God's promise to provide is true.

Our society emphasizes planning for the future by relying on what we can do for ourselves. Amid such a mind-set, it is important to remember that God fulfills His promise to provide for all our needs. Just as He fulfilled His promises to Elijah and the widow. Just as He fulfilled His promise to send His only Son to be our Savior.

Explain to your child that sometimes God uses people as He provides for the needs of others. Have your child help you select nonperishable food for your local food bank or clothing for a charity. Then take your child with you when you deliver the donations. In your prayers with your child, thank God for generously providingfor your physical needs, for giving you enough to share with others, and for keeping His promise to provide for your eternal needs by sending Christ, the Savior.

The Editor